W9-CMU-242

# SPEAK UP!
## CONFRONTING DISCRIMINATION IN YOUR DAILY LIFE™

# CONFRONTING
# CLASS
# DISCRIMINATION

## SHERRI MABRY GORDON

Rosen
YA™
New York

Published in 2018 by The Rosen Publishing Group, Inc.
29 East 21st Street, New York, NY 10010

Copyright © 2018 by The Rosen Publishing Group, Inc.

First Edition

All rights reserved. No part of this book may be reproduced in any form without permission in writing from the publisher, except by a reviewer.

**Library of Congress Cataloging-in-Publication Data**

Names: Gordon, Sherri Mabry, author.
Title: Confronting class discrimination / Sherri Mabry Gordon.
Description: New York : Rosen Publishing, 2018 | Series: Speak up! Confronting discrimination in your daily life | Audience: Grades 7–12. | Includes bibliographical references and index.
Identifiers: LCCN 2017017496| ISBN 9781538381700 (library bound) | ISBN 9781538381687 (pbk.) | ISBN 9781538381694 (6 pack)
Subjects: LCSH: Classism—United States—Juvenile literature. | Discrimination—United States—Juvenile literature.
Classification: LCC HN90.S6 G67 2017 | DDC 305.50973—dc23
LC record available at https://lccn.loc.gov/2017017496

*Manufactured in China*

# CONTENTS

# INTRODUCTION

**S**am* grew up in a rural community where most of his classmates came from similar economic backgrounds. In fact, he rarely noticed class discrimination until he went off to college. But while attending Ohio State University in Columbus, Ohio, he was forced to face the fact that he came from more modest means than some of his classmates.

"Looking back, high school was easy," Sam recalls. "We were all really about the same with some slight variances. But [class discrimination] really hit in college. Social activities, classes, jobs—the rich kids made an effort to make others feel inferior. The jobs I had in college had me working for rich people. They seemed to make a point to let you know the difference."

Even though Sam was one of only a few kids from his high school to attend college, he knew from a young age that he wanted to do more with his life than get a job and get married. He watched his older brothers get good grades and leave for college, and he planned to do the same.

"Back then, not a lot of kids went to college," Sam explains. "If I had been the oldest, I might [not have continued going to school.] But while it wasn't easy to pay for school, I had older siblings that lived the same life I did but were smarter than everyone else. I learned in elementary school that bank accounts had no effect on GPA. I wanted to be like my older brothers more than I wanted to be like anyone else."

Attending college as a low-income student comes with challenges. Many times, poorer students are excluded from clubs, events, and social activities because of income.

Today, Sam is a marketing and design professional living in an upper-middle-class suburb outside of Columbus, Ohio. Yet, he still notices how classism impacts those around him.

"It has gotten a lot worse," he says. "Maybe back then I was too naïve, but I still see [discrimination] in every aspect of life. The thing that stands out most is

The move from one social class to another is not always easy. Despite making more money and belonging to a higher class, many people who were once poor still experience discrimination.

that as [some] people climb a little, they feel the need to look down on those below them to make themselves feel better. I would like to say that is a bad generalization, but the exceptions are very few. I'm not sure where society came off the tracks."

*Please note that the interview source's name has been changed to protect his identity.*

# CHAPTER ONE

# WHAT IS CLASS DISCRIMINATION?

**R**ecall the story of the Disney film *Aladdin*. A young man is living on the streets. To survive, he steals food from the marketplace but dreams of escaping his life of poverty and living in a palace some-day. Meanwhile, a beautiful princess, Jasmine, is being forced into an arranged marriage in a nearby castle. Because she wants to marry for love and not based on wealth or class, she dresses as a peasant and flees the castle. Once in the marketplace, she meets Aladdin.

While they both realize they have a lot in common, they also know their class differences in society will prevent them from being together. It is not until Aladdin gets his hands on a magic lamp and wishes to be turned into a prince that they can finally be together. Although *Aladdin* is a classic "rags to riches" romance, it is also a clear illustration of classism and the barriers that exist between the wealthy and the poor.

As in the example above, it can be very difficult for the poor to cross barriers and have meaningful relationships with the wealthy. Even if two young people can move beyond or outside of the class barriers that would hold them back, others in their class may find their relationship hard to accept. What's more, despite

The Disney movie *Aladdin* is a classic "rags to riches" romance. It is also an example of classism and how the wealthy and poor interact. It is not a new story; *Aladdin* can be traced back to the *Arabian Nights* (c. ninth century).

advertising a positive message about class mobility, *Aladdin* suggestively perpetuates accepted stereotypes about the poor by displaying Aladdin as homeless and a thief.

## WHAT IS CLASSISM?

Classism, or class discrimination, is prejudice based on a person's social class. In other words, people are discriminated against or treated unfairly based on the class to which they belong. Typically, this means that the poor are often treated unfairly because of their lower position in society. Meanwhile, those in the higher classes typically have more power and privilege. In other words, people from lower social classes are excluded, devalued, and separated from others while those in the wealthy and middle classes have access to better education and more opportunities. This often results in extreme inequality among the rich and the poor.

To better understand classism, it is important to look at four basic types. These types include individual, institutional, cultural, and internalized classism. With individual classism, a person's thoughts or behaviors lead to discrimination based on social class. An example might be a woman who assumes that all people from a particular neighborhood are dangerous and immoral. As a result, she refuses to let her kids socialize with anyone from that neighborhood even though they attend the same school and are friends. When people allow stereotypes, opinions, or generalizations to impact their behavior toward a group of people, it is called classism.

Sometimes the laws and practices within a community create classism. This is called institutional classism. One example in the United States is that fact that the poor have little to no access to quality health care. Even though research shows they are often in greater need of health care services, health care organizations frequently do not open up in poorer neighborhoods. As a result, those in poverty are often forced to use emergency rooms as their only means of getting health care.

Meanwhile, cultural classism occurs when society promotes negative attitudes and beliefs about a social class. The Disney movie *Aladdin* is an example of cultural classism. Aladdin is portrayed as a thief and not worthy of the princess until he becomes a prince himself.

Finally, internalized classism occurs when a person living in poverty or as part of a lower social class internalizes beliefs about his or her social class. In return, this belief system not only impacts his or her future success but also affects his or her self-esteem.

# BRINGING CLASSISM TO THE FOREFRONT

Over the last several decades, the wealthiest 1 percent of Americans have more than doubled their share of the national income. Meanwhile, the bottom 80 percent have watched their share shrink. As a result, many Americans are struggling just to survive, especially with working class jobs moving overseas, the housing market crashing, and unemployment rising.

A group of people took notice of these issues and wanted to bring attention to the country's inequalities. In September 2011, a movement called Occupy Wall Street was kicked off in New York's financial district. The primary goal was to call attention to income inequality in the United States as well as greed, corruption, and the undue influence American corporations have on government. The movement, which received global attention, stood behind the idea: "We are the 99 percent." This slogan

The slogan "We are the 99 percent" calls attention to income inequality. Most people are not part of the 1 percent of Americans that control most of the nation's wealth.

communicated that income inequality exists between the wealthiest 1 percent and the rest of the population.

While protesting, the group brought widespread attention to classism and inequality in the United States. But just a few months later, they were forced out of the Wall Street area. In turn, they began to occupy banks, corporate headquarters, board meetings, foreclosed homes, and college campuses. Eventually, they stopped protesting and their website is no longer being managed. But while it existed, the movement was extremely successful at bringing attention to income inequality in the United States.

## HISTORY OF CLASSISM

When settlers first came to America from European nations, they were looking for religious freedom; they also brought with them the idea of property and ownership. Even though many of them had been oppressed, they still knew no other way of establishing their communities.

It is, therefore, not surprising that the new government gave a voice to property owners. What's more, the newcomers felt they were superior to the Native Americans who were already living in the area. Although they knew what it was like to feel oppressed themselves, it was not long before they began taking land away from and oppressing the natives. Eventually, white, male property owners became the elite in the new American colonies. Their wealth gave them the ability to control the government. And they used this privilege to maintain the rights of property owners and to establish order.

Today, the social classes are fairly well-defined. Yet to many people the issue of classism does not exist. Many believe that poor people are stuck in their situations because of their own bad life choices, lack of intelligence, and laziness. This failure by most people to recognize classism does not make it any less real.

## THE TALE OF TWO BELIEFS

Everyone has heard of the American dream: if you work hard enough, you can achieve anything. Ironically, this belief in the American dream often leads to class discrimination. When people are not able to pull themselves out of poverty or cross over into a higher class, people may assume that they just are not working hard enough. This belief is rooted in a system known as a meritocracy. Meritocracy assumes that people in lower classes are somehow inferior and less talented than those in higher classes.

The problem with believing in a meritocracy is that it makes it very difficult to see class inequality. What's more, it leads people to believe that we all have the same opportunities and can achieve anything if we set our minds to it. But that is simply not the case. For instance, not everyone has access to a quality education. And without a quality education, finding a quality job is challenging.

Many people also believe that poor people are to blame for their problems. In other words, they believe that the poor are less intelligent or not as talented as others. When people buy into this belief system, they are believing in deficit theory. The deficit theory exists because people form their opinions about poor people based on stereotypes. They also tend to ignore systems that reinforce the cycle of poverty. In general, the deficit theory is a victim-blaming belief.

## BORN TO BE POOR?

Research shows that if you are born poor in the United States, you are very likely to remain that way. A recent Harvard and University of California study tried to determine if America is really the land of opportunity.

In other words, can poor children escape their neighborhoods and make a better life for themselves? Sadly, the answer is not very often. In fact, barely one in ten children will escape poverty even in socially mobile cities like Salt Lake City, Utah, and San Francisco, California. And in some cities, only one out of twenty-five children will find their way out of poverty.

This lack of mobility is related to the types of schools these students attend, says Christine Boucher, Director of the Center for Groveport Madison Human Needs. Her organization provides emergency assistance in the Groveport Madison area in Ohio. They help people with rent, car repairs, medical bills, and utilities.

"So many people say that education is the way out of poverty. But a lot of these kids attend neighborhood schools that are poorly funded," she explains. "They do not have access to the technology and science equipment that other, wealthier schools have. What's more, a lot of these kids just do not value education and drop out of school because that is what their parents did."

According to Boucher, many people living in poverty are born into it. This is called generational poverty. In generational poverty, kids learn how to cope with their situation by observing their parents and others in their neighborhood.

But some people are poor because of a situation that occurred in their lives, Boucher says. This is called situational poverty. People in situational poverty may have lost their job or had a serious family illness that caused them to lose everything. As a result, they are learning how to adjust now that they are in a different social class.

The classic '80s movie *Pretty In Pink* highlights the challenges poor students often face in high school. In the movie, Andie, a high school senior, lives with her underemployed working-class father but falls in love with a "richie" named Blane. Throughout the movie, Andie is harassed and bullied by the arrogant rich kids. In the end, though, love triumphs over social class.

"They are living paycheck to paycheck, earning just enough money to keep from going under," she explains. "Others are out of work and searching for a new job while relying on other means like unemployment, food stamps, and food banks."

According to Boucher, a person's class determines a lot about the person, including their eating habits, speech patterns, and their family relationships.

As a result, the transition from one social class to another—or social mobility, as it is sometimes called—impacts a person's identity. For instance, many habits, thoughts, and beliefs are specific to each social class. And moving from one class to another requires that the person learn how to exist in their new social class.

"If someone is born into poverty," Boucher adds, "it is very hard for them to find their way out and if they do find their way out, they have to give up a lot to get there. Many times, their relationships with families and friends will suffer because of the change."

# MYTHS AND FACTS

**MYTH**
People in poverty are lazy.

Fact
People in poverty are usually good problem solvers with very limited resources. They also may not have the necessary knowledge, education, social skills, or transportation to be employed.

**MYTH**
Lower income families are mostly found in urban areas.

Fact
Poverty is just as prominent in rural areas and even in suburban communities.

**MYTH**
Lower class people are not as intelligent as people in other social classes.

Fact
Intelligence is not measured by how much money a person has. However, poorer students have fewer resources and opportunities. As a result, they do not always reach their academic potential.

# CHAPTER TWO

# WHAT IMPACT DOES CLASSISM HAVE?

**B**efore they reach their fourth birthday, kids in the United States from wealthy families will have heard as many as thirty million more words than those from low-income or poor families, according to researchers. This phenomenon is often called a "word gap" and it has a huge impact on the future earning potential of kids.

In fact, numerous studies have found that a child's exposure to words and books is often directly tied to their income level. In other words, poor families often cannot afford books and are so busy trying to meet day-to-day needs that they do not have time for lengthy or enriching conversations. What's more, they are often trapped in neighborhoods with poor-performing schools, poorly-funded libraries, and low graduation rates. As a result, the deck is stacked against them from the beginning.

## CLASSISM AND EDUCATION

By the time children start school, researchers say there is already a two-year gap between kids from poor families and the rest of the student population. By the time they reach third grade, there is a three-year difference.

"A lot of times what happens is that the poor are just trying to meet basic needs so education often takes a backseat to earning a living," says Beth Urban, Director of Education for the Homeless Families Foundation. "They also do not have access to extra services like tutoring or homework help programs because no one has a car. No one has the time either; and they do not have the money to pay for it if costs money."

Additionally, resources like after-school tutoring, enrichment programs, and PTO support are more readily available in wealthier areas than they are in poorer communities, adds Christine Boucher. "Better funded schools also have more experienced teachers and smaller classrooms. And they tend to have more computer equipment as well as up-to-date textbooks."

Middle income and wealthy children often have books in their homes and are exposed to more words before they start school. Poor children may not have this luxury, leading them to suffer from a "word gap" in school.

It is not surprising that well-off school districts have higher rates of high school graduation and college attendance. And research shows that students from more well-off school districts are accepted into more selective colleges. But according to experts this is not based on their ability as much as it is on their family's income. For instance, 82 percent of wealthy students with SAT scores of more than 1200 graduate from college. But only 44 percent of low-income students with the same high scores will advance equally far. It is not that these students are not smart enough, it is that their family just doesn't have enough money to sustain college attendance.

What's more, studies show that millions of qualified high school students are not even attending college. The reasons are simple: either they cannot afford it or the college admissions policy screens them out. For instance, many colleges are looking for students with a lot of extracurricular activities and unique experiences; young people from lower social classes simply may not have been able to afford to participate in these types of extracurriculars.

If a student is the oldest child in his or her family, he or she probably has had to handle the child care or get a job to help pay the bills, Urban says. Students from lower income families also tend to have less access to the internet. They cannot afford a computer and often do not have internet set up in the home. They also are not able to take trips, study abroad, or participate in unpaid internships. They simply have not had the time or the resources to devote to education or new experiences, Urban says.

Many experts wonder if colleges are so focused on ethnic and racial diversity that they are overlooking applicants with less privileged backgrounds. For instance, studies of the nation's top undergraduate schools show that three-quarters of students are from

Students from lower income families often have limited access to the internet. They also cannot afford a computer and often do not have the time or the resources to devote to education.

the country's top income bracket. Meanwhile, less than 10 percent are from the bottom income bracket. Likewise, more than half of the bachelor's degrees in the United States were earned by students with family incomes of about $98,000. But only 9.4 percent of bachelor's degrees were earned by students with family incomes below $33,000.

## CLASSISM AND FOOD

In the United States, there is a growing trend for healthy eating. Whether it is eating whole foods or clean eating, there is a general consensus that eating nutritious food is important. But eating healthy food is not cheap. As a result, it is extremely difficult for lower class or poor families to eat healthy food.

To make matters worse, many people from middle and upper classes pass judgment on how the poor feed their families. "It is not uncommon to hear statements like: 'Why does she feed her kids that junk?' 'I cannot believe she is feeding her kid McDonald's. Have they never seen a vegetable?'" says Boucher. Simply put, fast food and processed foods are cheaper than fresh fruits and vegetables.

For the poor, fast food is often cheaper than fresh fruits and vegetables. Plus, lack of transportation makes it hard to get to the grocery store. As a result, many poor families rely on fast food to feed their families.

Additionally, lower income families may not have adequate transportation to get to grocery stores. Many poor neighborhoods have convenience stores, where the food is overpriced, instead of supermarkets, says Boucher. And for some, even if they can get to a grocery store, they may not have the storage space to keep fresh foods. Perhaps their refrigerator no longer works or they are living in an extended stay facility that does not have refrigeration or a stove.

## CLASSISM AND HEALTH

Aside from unhealthy eating, there also is a link between poverty and poor health. Although poor health among low-income populations has long been recognized as an issue, research now demonstrates that class discrimination also plays a role in causing poor health. When teens experience discrimination, the stress of that experience eventually leads to poorer health. Even subtle forms of discrimination can have an impact, according to a study led by a University of Wisconsin researcher Dr. Thomas Fuller-Rowell.

"Experiences of discrimination are often subtle rather than blatant and the exact reason for unfair treatment is often not clear to the victim," says Dr. Fuller-Rowell. Yet, this perceived discrimination still leaves an impression. He found that the poorer an individual is, the more he or she experiences perceived discrimination, and the worse his or her health is.

Meanwhile, a Stress in America Survey found that people who have dealt with discrimination rate their stress levels higher than those who have not been discriminated against. What's more, discrimination has been linked to depression, anxiety, high blood pressure, obesity, and substance abuse.

It can even be stressful just belonging to a group that is discriminated against, even if the person never experiences discrimination firsthand. As a result, it is not uncommon for the anticipation of discrimination to lead people to avoid situations where they might be treated poorly. This can cause the individual to miss out on educational and job opportunities.

## CLASSISM AND EMPLOYMENT

"Students from lower socioeconomic classes are also less informed about the types of employment that are available," says Urban. "When you ask a kid what he wants to be when he grows up, he usually knows the basics like a doctor, lawyer, fireman, policeman, and so on," she says. "Because his school never offered a class like microbiology, he has no idea that there are chemical engineers or what they might do. They have not had the experiences or the worldview to see anything different."

The lack of adequate transportation to get to and from a job is another issue the poor must wrestle with, says Boucher. Some poorer neighborhoods do not have access to public transportation. And without a reliable car, people in these neighborhoods are not able to work because the walk is often too long and unsafe.

"Of course, there are some employers that will work with them, but in general many employers see lower income workers as disposable," she says. "They do

In many poor neighborhoods, classes such as computer programming and microbiology are rarely offered. As a result, students do not realize there are more career opportunities than those to which they have been exposed.

not have a lot of compassion for maintaining anyone. Overall, they are not interested in hearing what they can provide to the workers to help them keep their jobs."

For some of the working poor, it can be expensive just to keep their jobs. Take Joanne, who works as an administrative assistant. She must make a 60-mile round trip commute every day to get to work. Her car needs to be repaired, but she simply does not have the money to fix it. If her car dies, she will likely lose her job and be in a financial crisis. Without the ability to finance a new car, she is taking a risk every time she drives to work.

# UNDERSTANDING THE WORKING CLASS

More often than not, people think that the working class and the poor are the same. Politicians in particular confuse these groups. But there are some very clear distinctions between the working class and the poor in the United States. According to the Pew Research Center, the poor make up about 29 percent of the population while the working or middle class, as it is sometimes called, makes up about 48 percent. The remaining 21 percent is comprised of upper class.

Years ago, two out of three Americans were considered middle class. Now, with jobs hard to come by and more people falling below the poverty line, the Pew Research Center says the middle class will soon become the minority. Most available jobs are given to upper class Americans with college degrees. As a result, working class citizens struggle to find jobs that would allow them to maintain the middle-class lifestyles they desire. Many have a hard time just making ends meet.

The working class and the poor differ in other ways as well. As their name implies, members of the working class are employed; if not, they are actively looking for work. They also usually have a high school education and sometimes a degree from a trade school. Recently, many members of the working class have had trouble finding steady, full-time jobs. More and more manufacturers who previously employed people from the working class have moved their operations overseas. What's more, people in this group often do not qualify for programs that the poor qualify for like food stamps, health care rebates, and child-care programs. As a result, they often have a deep resentment toward the poor in the United States.

Joan Williams, author of *White Working Class* and Distinguished Professor of Law at the University of California, explains: "My sister-in-law worked full-time for Head Start, providing free child care for poor women while earning so little she almost couldn't pay for her own. She resented this, especially the fact that some of the kids' moms did not work. One [mom] arrived late one day to pick up her child, carrying shopping bags from Macy's. My sister-in-law was livid."

# CLASSISM AND SOCIAL INTERACTION

Researchers have discovered that social status impacts not just how much money people make, the kinds of cars they drive, or the schools they attend. Class may also reveal things about how people think, feel, and act. In fact, according to an article in *Psychological Review,* researchers discovered that the lower someone's social class, the more they tend to believe that uncontrollable forces and other people have power over their lives. Success, to them, involves learning to read others.

Meanwhile, they found that the more resources someone has, the more self-focused they are. Higher income people also tend to believe that they have genes that make them more able to succeed. They also feel more entitled and are more narcissistic. Some researchers believe that this sense of entitlement leads people from higher classes to act more selfishly and less ethically than those of lower income classes. They also tend to disconnect from others' concerns or needs.

By contrast, people from lower income classes tend to be more emotionally aware of other people's needs. They also are better at reading emotions on people's faces and are more generous and helpful than their wealthier peers.

# CHAPTER THREE

# HOW ARE PEOPLE DISCRIMINATED AGAINST?

In a YouTube video called "Fare Evasion," a man dressed in a tuxedo attempts to board a bus without a ticket. He tells the bus driver that he lost his ticket or that he forgot his wallet. Each time he tries to board a bus, the driver responds kindly and allows him to ride the bus without question.

Later, the same man dresses poorly and attempts to board the bus with the same excuses. Each time he is denied. At one point, one bus driver laughs at him. Even when the man approaches the same bus driver who had been kind to him when he was wearing a tuxedo, he is refused a ride.

This video illustrates the harsh reality of how people who are poor or from a lower social class are treated differently than those who are rich or powerful. When dressed in shabby clothes the man in this video was perceived to be poor, lying, and trying to get something for free. However, the same man dressed in a tuxedo was viewed as a rich man who was telling the truth.

*Pretty Woman* (1990) illustrates the concept that people are treated differently based on the way they dress. In the movie, Vivian is treated well when people don't know how she has made her living. They respect her when they're visually dazzled.

# METHODS OF BIAS

It is not uncommon for people to make judgments about others simply based on the way they look, dress, act, and talk. While most people can recognize the obvious ways in which people are discriminated against, there are some more subtle forms of discrimination that may go unnoticed. For instance, poorer students who attend school in the suburbs often face challenges that some of their wealthier classmates take for granted.

Beth Urban suggests the people should consider the following barriers facing poor students:

*Inability to afford fees for athletics, music, band, theatre, and more.* Unless the school provides scholarships or waives pay-to-participate fees for poorer students, these fees may keep some students from participating in extracurricular activities.

*Less access to school supplies, especially when the lists are lengthy.* Students may not be able to afford the items that schools and teachers request for school. If a student arrives to school without all the necessary supplies, this can create a negative perception of the student in the teacher's mind right from the start.

*No money for tennis shoes or equipment needed for sports and other extracurricular activities.* Many times, families have to decide whether they are going to pay for shoes or for school supplies. Often, they cannot afford to pay for both.

*No access to vacations and other destination experiences outside of the immediate community.* When students lack these experiences, they may not have the same scope of reference as others in their school. This can have a negative impact on the papers they write and the tests they take.

*More likely to be moved during redistricting.* Many schools engage in redistricting, especially in the suburbs, as a way to even out their school populations and sometimes to ensure they have a set number of students on free and reduced lunch at each school. As a result, the poorer students in the district are often the ones moved. They are pulled away from their communities and their friends and placed with kids who are nothing like them.

Many experts believe that standardized testing is discriminatory. Test questions are often developed assuming that all children have the same worldview. Poor children often haven't had the experiences described in the test questions.

Even standardized testing is discriminatory against the poor, according to Urban. "The questions have no concept of what inner city kids are struggling with and what might be within their frame of reference," she says. "If a test question involves the word island, this is an extremely challenging question for a poor student who has no context for what an island might be like. They have never visited an island. They haven't seen one. How can they know how to answer the question if they cannot even draw a picture in their mind?"

Another example Urban offers is the basic pre-kindergarten assessment that she often uses with students in her program. "I had one little boy who had never experienced an umbrella, a cow, or a deer. So when we were going through the 'Ready Set Read' program, he could not possibly know what those things are."

## HOW DISCRIMINATION FEELS

According to the American Psychological Association, discrimination of any type is becoming a public health issue. Studies show that class discrimination heightens stress levels. Even people who have never been directly discriminated against can feel the impact. It is stressful simply being a member of a social class that is often discriminated against.

Overall, people who have experienced class discrimination report feeling like they are not welcome in certain situations. They also report feeling judged and looked down on, as well not knowing whom they can trust.

Some common feelings that class discrimination causes include:

- Feeling isolated or like an outsider even in one's own school or workplace
- Having pressure to prove oneself and defy stereotypes
- Being unsure or confused about whether or not the treatment one receives is because of one's social class or something else entirely
- Feeling defeated and often living out the stereotypes because people do not expect more
- Considering dropping out, transferring, or quitting work or school
- Experiencing fear, anxiety, depression, and anger because of one's situation

# TAKING OUT THE "WHITE TRASH"

One of the most overt examples of class discrimination is the use of the term "white trash." When people hear the term, they often think of poor whites living in rundown homes with too many kids and not enough government assistance. It's an insult given to whites who have not made it to the middle class or above. And according to director John Waters, it is "the last racist thing you can say and get away with."

Historians claim the term "white trash" arose in the 1820s in the Baltimore, Maryland, area. In fact, they believe the term was originally coined by African Americans of the time, both free and enslaved. Black people in this region were competing with poorer whites, most likely Irish immigrants and other semi-skilled workers, for the same jobs. The term reflected the hostilities between these social groups.

But it was the middle-class whites and the wealthy whites who made "white trash" a popular part of American speech. In 1854, Harriet Beecher Stowe devoted an entire chapter to the "Poor White Trash" in her book *Key to Uncle Tom's Cabin*.

This photo of a coal miner and his family in Bertha Hill, West Virginia, was taken in 1938. They would have been a common example of poor whites, people termed "white trash" by middle and upper classes.

*(continued on the next page)*

*(continued from the previous page)*

Most believed that people labeled white trash were not only living trashy lifestyles and having too many children, but that their bloodlines were also seriously defective. Some even speculated that people labeled white trash were inbred and should be prohibited from having any more children. As a result, some elitists wanted to put an end to this "white blemish."

Between 1907 and 1927, more than eight thousand involuntary sterilizations were performed on men and women. The thought behind these sterilizations was that the country was becoming racially polluted by these people and that they were unfit for reproduction. By May 1927, the Supreme Court ruled that the involuntary sterilization of Carrie Buck was permissible in the *Buck vs. Bell* case in Virginia. Without sterilization, any children Buck had would later become burdens of the state. Another sixty thousand Americans, most of them poor and indigent women, were sterilized without their consent.

Most involuntary sterilizations ended in the mid-1950s, but there were still reported cases well into the 1980s. It was not until 2002 that the state of Virginia admitted its mistake and apologized to the Buck family. California, which was responsible for the largest number of sterilizations, also apologized to the families who were impacted.

Today, the term "white trash" is still widely used, especially by other whites who look down on those who are not as successful. And many experts worry that people may try to use advances in genetic science to eliminate those considered white trash from the population.

## CHECK YOURSELF—ARE YOUR BELIEFS CLASSIST?

A lot of people have the wrong views about the poor in their community, according to Urban. People may visit the local shelter and want to volunteer or take part in their programs, but they have incorrect notions about what it means to be poor. Many, she says, are unintentionally classist in their views.

"I have a lot of conversations with people who want to know what poor kids look like," she says. "I tell them to look in the mirror. People who are poor do not

This seemingly average teenager enjoys listening to her iPod and journaling— except she is homeless and had been living in this shelter for over three months after her mother stole money she had set aside for college.

look any different from you and me. What makes them different are their struggles and the resources available to them."

She also says that people sometimes want to volunteer with their kids for all the wrong reasons. "People often want their kids to come volunteer so they know how good they have it. They aren't necessarily interested in helping the poor but instead are interested in proving a point. They also want to feel good while doing something for poor children."

These motivations are very self-focused and subtly classist. Urban says that people need to understand the issues surrounding the poor and lower class.

"Do not believe the myths that the poor are lazy and do not want to work. These are simply not true," she says. "Once you are in poverty it is much harder to move up. So many things are stacked against you. The best thing people can do is build some awareness of what people of lower social classes struggle with every day." Doing so might give them a new appreciation for what the poor and working class have to deal with.

"They are faced with a lot of barriers," Urban stresses. "Many times, the poor have no leisure time. They are working multiple jobs to make ends meet. And they have the chronic stress of living in poverty. Their focus is always on meeting basic needs to the point that they rarely can think of anything else."

# CHAPTER FOUR

# TAKING A STAND AGAINST CLASSISM

Paul Piff, PhD, a professor at the University of California, begins all of his classes the same way: he asks the students about their purchasing habits. Where do they shop? Is it JC Penney or Neiman Marcus? What do they use for transportation? The bus, a car, or the train? What is their favorite breakfast? Do they stop at Starbucks for a fruit smoothie or grab a donut at Dunkin' Donuts? He believes that as people go about their day, every decision they make is influenced by their social class.

"Class [also] affects whether someone is going to be accepted into a particular kind of school, their likelihood of succeeding in that school, the kinds of jobs they have access to, and the kinds of friends they make," he says in an American Psychological Association article. As a result, it is crucial that people have a solid understanding of the differences between classes so that the gap between the rich and poor can be bridged.

## CHALLENGE CLASSISM IN YOUR OWN LIFE

Experts say one of the best ways to build a bridge between the rich and the poor is to make changes in

Every decision a person makes is influenced by class. In the movie *Clueless*, the writers take a satirical look at what it means to be ultra-wealthy teenagers in America, including their shopping habits.

your own life first. Here are some ways in which you can challenge classism in your own life:

Examine your reactions to others. Do you make assumptions about a person's intelligence based on how they dress or what they look like? Are you afraid of poor or homeless people and assume they are dangerous?

Create an inclusive environment. Are you building friendships with people in different social classes and making an effort to find some common ground? Do you look people in the eye and acknowledge their humanity? Are you making every effort to be accepting and supportive even though you may be different?

Reject myths and stereotypes about poverty and the poor. Are you making assumptions about people before talking with them? Are you challenging others who make broad generalizations and classist remarks? Do you interrupt when someone is telling a classist joke or making a rude comment?

Be respectful of others. Do you believe that no matter how someone looks, dresses, acts, or speaks they deserve respect? Are you buying into the idea that poor people are less valued than others? Are you striving to treat everyone—regardless of class—with respect and compassion?

## STAND UP TO DISCRIMINATION BY BECOMING AN ADVOCATE

Once you have challenged classism in your own life, you may want to consider being an advocate for the poor in your own communities. Typically, an advocate does not belong to a lower social class him or herself, but supports and helps that social class. Here are some suggestions on how you can become an advocate:

Educate yourself about the issues. While you do not have to have a degree in sociology to advocate for the poor and the working classes, you should learn about the issues impacting the groups you want to support. One way you can do that is to examine how privilege, power, and classist beliefs have impacted others' lives as well as your own.

Realize that you will make mistakes. When classism is part of the culture, it is hard not to absorb some of its beliefs, attitudes, and opinions. No matter how hard you try, there may be times when you will say or do something that hurts someone else. When this happens, be willing to listen and to apologize when necessary. Sometimes admitting you were wrong can go a long way.

Challenge behaviors, not people. Remember, when you accuse someone of class discrimination, you are putting them on the defensive and they will be less likely to listen to what you have to say. Instead, try to start a thoughtful conversation about classism without making accusations.

Speak for yourself, not for others. It is important to say something when you witness classism. But at the

New York mayor Bill de Blasio meets with social worker Irwin Jeffrey, who has expressed concern over issues of gentrification and rising rents in his Brooklyn neighborhood. Advocates in positions of authority need to be prepared to listen.

same time, you need to avoid trying to speak for others. While you may have a good idea about what they are feeling or experiencing, you also run the risk of being wrong or appearing condescending. Instead, focus on sharing your own opinions, viewpoints, and research.

## HOW TO RECOGNIZE CLASS DISCRIMINATION

Sometimes class discrimination is easy to recognize. But there are times when the person discriminating against you or others can be very subtle. You know what they are saying or doing doesn't feel right, you just don't know for sure that it's discrimination. You may have witnessed this behavior, or have been a target of it yourself. Luckily, there are ways to recognize class discrimination, both at school and in the broader community.

You are being discriminated against if:
- you have to defend who you are or what you believe;
- you feel like you have to explain why you or your group is different;
- your teacher, boss, or classmate acts superior and condescending;
- your comments about your personal experiences are belittled;
- your teacher, boss, or classmate acts like they do not trust you for no apparent reason; or
- your teacher, boss, or classmate quickly changes the subject when you walk in the room.

## FIVE THINGS VICTIMS OF DISCRIMINATION SHOULD NEVER DO

Discrimination is a painful experience that can leave a lasting impact. For this reason, it is not something you should brush under the rug or try to bury inside. If you are a victim of class discrimination, it is important that you find healthy ways to cope with your feelings.

Healthy coping mechanisms are important to your overall well-being. Likewise, ignoring your feelings or pretending like class discrimination did not hurt can have a negative impact on you. Here are some ways to stand up to discrimination:

One way people come to terms with poverty is to write or journal about it. In her memoir, *The Glass Castle*, Jeannette Wells shares how her parents' lifestyle decisions affected her own values as a child.

Do not dwell on your situation. When you have been discriminated against, it is very hard to shake it off. After all, what someone said or did to you really hurts. But you cannot let their words and actions control you. Remember, you cannot control what other people say or do, but you can control your response. And the worst thing you can do is to think about what happened over and over again. In fact, researchers have found that dwelling on negative experiences causes more stress and anxiety than the initial experience. Instead, focus on the positives in your life and not what someone else thinks.

Do not embrace what other people say about you. Classism has the potential to define you, if you allow it. Instead, remind yourself of who you really are. Fill your life with people who encourage you and try to avoid the people who would like to tear you down.

Do not compromise who you are in order to fit in. Never try to be someone that you are not. Instead, be proud of who you are. It is much easier to be authentic than it is try to be someone that you are not. In fact, pretending can be pretty exhausting. Remember, there is only one you and you should be proud of that person. Do not let someone shame you for who you are.

Do not blame yourself. Too often, when young people are discriminated against, they feel like they somehow deserve it. But that is simply not true. Class discrimination is a choice that another person makes. Instead of blaming yourself for allowing it to impact your sense of self-worth, place the responsibility back on the shoulders of those discriminating against you. Do not be afraid to hold others accountable for their actions.

Do not isolate yourself. When you are discriminated against, it is natural to want to avoid your friends, school, and work. But when you do, you are just hurting yourself. Isolating yourself will not protect you from further pain. Seek out friends and family members who you can rely upon. They will remind you of your value and your worth.

# CHAPTER FIVE

# ENDING CLASSISM IN YOUR EVERYDAY LIFE

There is no doubt that racism is a serious problem in this country. But most classism experts argue that class discrimination is just as big of an issue. They feel we should talk about it as much as we discuss race issues.

"When you look at the data, the most [harmful] problem ... today is [the difference between] the haves and have nots," says Heather Long, an editor at CNNMoney who wrote an opinion piece for the *Guardian*. "Race plays a factor, but middle class blacks live fairly similar lives to middle class whites. Middle class blacks and middle class whites work together. Their children have playdates and go to the same prep schools and colleges. What you are far less likely to see is a lower income child of any race mixing with a middle or upper income child."

A survey from the Pew Research Center says that the income gap in the United States is viewed as a bigger source of conflict than race, age, or national origin. So how do we get children of different income levels to interact with one another?

Many say the answer lies in getting people of different classes to form relationships with one another.

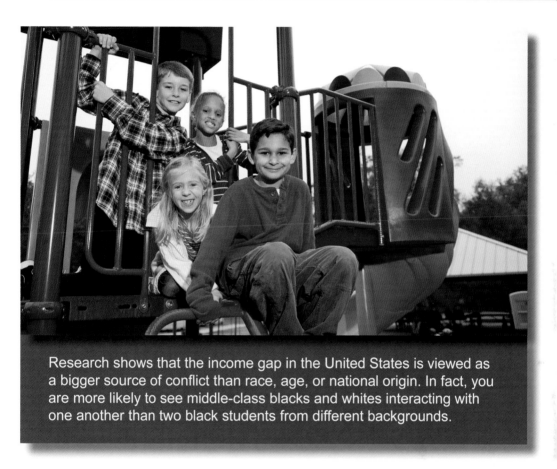

Research shows that the income gap in the United States is viewed as a bigger source of conflict than race, age, or national origin. In fact, you are more likely to see middle-class blacks and whites interacting with one another than two black students from different backgrounds.

The problem is that most people are more comfortable interacting with others who are just like them. And when relationships do develop across social classes, there can be a higher risk for misunderstanding and tension.

## THE PROBLEM WITH STAYING IN YOUR LANE

Comedian Kevin Hart joked once that he stays in his own financial lane—he does not get out of his lane and mingle with others who are in different social classes.

As a rule, this is true of most people. They tend to hang out with people who are like them in some way. They might have similar educational backgrounds, interests, incomes, and occupations. But for class discrimination to end, people need to step outside of their comfort zones, says Urban.

"People need to face their fears over the poor and the lower social classes," she adds. "A lot of people base their opinions and beliefs on the movies they have watched. As a result, they have this perception of what poverty is like and how dangerous lower income neighborhoods are. The first step in combatting classism is facing those fears."

"We cannot end classism until people make an effort to develop relationships with others," she adds. "Sometimes the first step is being aware that there are differences between stereotypes and reality." Once that is known, people can work on bridging the gap between classes.

## END VICTIM BLAMING

One way that classism is perpetuated is by blaming the poor for their circumstances. This is a kind of victim blaming. Many people engage in victim blaming by asserting that the poor do not make sound financial decisions, are not intelligent, and do not work hard enough. To keep from engaging in victim blaming yourself, you should familiarize yourself with some common ways in which people blame the poor for their circumstances.

"He should change." Many times, people will point out what is wrong with the poor rather than recognizing that the real problem lies with classism and unequal opportunities. Instead, people find it easier to tell a poor person how he should change in order to move out of poverty. While there are certain life skills that people in lower social classes may need to learn—budgeting,

Oprah Winfrey lived in poverty growing up—first in rural Mississippi and then in inner-city Milwaukee. Winfrey overcame these circumstances, defying the expectations of victim blaming with hard work and perseverence to achieve a net worth of over $3 billion in 2017.

*(continued on the next page)*

*(continued from the previous page)*

time management, and other employment skills, for instance—lacking these skills is never an excuse for classist treatment.

"He caused it or brought it on himself." Many times, the poor are caught in a vicious cycle of poverty. Yet many people believe their situation is of their own making. This is not always the case. Many children are born into poverty and struggle hard to get out. Being born in a poor neighborhood makes it extremely difficult for children to get a good education and enroll in college. It is unfair to assume they could be doing something to change their situation overnight.

"He should have known better." When people see something unfortunate happen to a poor person, they usually assume that he or she made a poor choice. But the fact is that people should have the freedom to move about in the world without fear of being judged for everything they do. Instead of blaming a poor person for living in poverty and assuming they did something to cause it, people should take the time to extend a helping hand.

## EXPAND YOUR CIRCLE

If you want to break down the barriers between classes, start by becoming more inclusive of others who are different from you. Expanding your circle of friends will not only enrich your life, but you also will gain a more realistic perspective of the challenges that other social classes face. Here are some steps you can follow to become a more inclusive person in your school and at work:

Begin by examining yourself. Take a look at your neighborhood, your school, and your friendships. Then be honest. Do you have friends from different social classes? What about different races and religions? Are you accepting of people or do you belong to a clique? Do you make judgments and maintain stereotypes? If you want to have an impact on classism, you need to need to be open to diverse relationships.

Work hard on being inclusive. Remember that classism makes people feel excluded. From being isolated in the lunchroom and ignored during class to being excluded from after-school events, exclusion is

In the classic movie *The Breakfast Club*, five students meet in detention. They learn that judgments based on appearance, income level, and speech patterns are not always true and that they have more in common than they would have imagined.

one of the most painful types of classism someone will experience. In fact, research suggests that being excluded impacts a person's self-worth and identity.

Embrace differences. Avoid making judgments about a person's appearance, income level, and speech patterns. Once you recognize that everyone has something to offer, you will be less likely to exclude others based on their differences.

Strive to be an advocate, not a bystander. Peer pressure is a powerful social regulator. But so is standing up for other people. Remember, everyone has something to offer the world. The best way to break down barriers and put an end to classism is to find out what that something is and celebrate it.

# 10 GREAT QUESTIONS
## TO ASK A SCHOOL COUNSELOR

1. How can I tell if I am being discriminated against?

2. Where (else) can I go to get help?

3. How can I get the discrimination to stop?

4. Is there any way to get people to accept me for who I am?

5. Why does classism hurt so much?

6. Is there something wrong with me?

7. Why do people care so much about money?

8. Why do some students judge others for the way they dress or speak?

9. Where do you think classism occurs in this school?

10. What do you think students at this school should do about classism?

# GLOSSARY

**advocate**  A person who supports the cause of another.

**classism**  Prejudice or discrimination based on a person's social class.

**deficit theory**  The belief that the lower class lack the intelligence and skills to succeed.

**entitlement**  The belief that a person or a group of people deserve special treatment.

**food insecurity**  The state in which a family or individual does not have access to enough food during any given period of time.

**generational poverty**  A term used to describe families that have lived in poverty for at least two generations.

**income inequality**  The unequal distribution of income across an entire country compared to the population.

**indigent**  An older word used to describe someone suffering from extreme poverty.

**meritocracy**  A system in which the talented are chosen and moved ahead on the basis of their achievement.

**narcissism**  A term used by psychologists to identify people who display extreme selfishness, a craving for admiration, and an inflated view of their own talents.

**Occupy Wall Street**  A protest movement designed to bring attention to income inequality that began in the financial district of New York City, known as Wall Street, in September 2011.

**privilege**  A special advantage that certain groups of people have been granted; wealthy people typically have more privilege than poor people.

**situational poverty**  A period of time when families or individuals fall below the poverty line due to a situation in their lives such as illness, job loss, or divorce.

**social mobility**  The movement of families or individuals from one class to another; usually the term is used to describe upward movement.

**socioeconomic**  Relates to the influence that both finances and education have on a person's social class.

**stereotype**  A commonly accepted view or opinion about an individual or group of individuals.

**victim blaming**  Holding the victim responsible for the injustices that have occurred in his or her life.

**white trash**  A racist and derogatory term that is used to describe poor white people.

**word gap**  A term coined by researchers to explain the language and learning differences between the richest children and the poorest children based on how many words they know.

**working class**  A group of people in society who are employed primarily in manual labor and industrial jobs.

# FOR MORE INFORMATION

Center on Budget and Policy Priorities
820 First Street NE, Suite 510
Washington, DC 20002
(202) 408-1080
Website: http://www.cbpp.org
Facebook: @centeronbudget
Twitter: @centeronbudget
Instagram: @centeronbudget
YouTube: @centeronbudget
This organization is one of the nation's top policy
   organizations. Its primary purpose is to conduct
   research and ensure that the needs of low-income
   families and individuals are considered during
   proposed budget and tax policies.

DoSomething.org
19 West 21st Street, 8th Floor
New York, NY 10010
Email: donate@dosomething.org
Website: http://www.dosomething.org
Facebook: @dosomething
Twitter: @dosomething
Instagram: @dosomething
YouTube: @DoSomething1
DoSomething.org is an online social movement that
   encourages young people to do something good in
   their communities. Once a young person develops a
   campaign, it is posted on the website so that others
   can join the cause.

Ontario Association of Food Banks
555 Richmond Street West, Suite 501
Toronto, ON M5V 3B1
Canada
(416) 656-4100
Website: https://oafb.ca
Facebook: @OntarioFoodBanks
Twitter: @OAFB
The primary goal of this association is to provide food
banks with food and resources. They also provide
ideas and solutions that help address food insecurity.

Statistics Canada
150 Tunney's Pasture Driveway
Ottawa, ON K1A 0T6
Canada
(800) 263-1136
Website: http://www.statcan.gc.ca
Statistics Canada is designed to produce statistics
that help Canadians better understand life in
Canada such as its society, population, economy,
and resources. They believe providing statistics is a
federal responsibility and regularly have as many as
350 active surveys at any given time.

Teaching for Change
PO Box 73038
Washington, DC 20056
(800) 763-9131
Website: http://www.teachingforchange.org
Facebook: @TeachingForChange
Twitter: @teachingchange
YouTube: @teachingforchange

This educational organization empowers teachers and students to question and rethink the world outside the classroom. The goal is to equip students with the ability to create a more equitable society while becoming good global citizens.

The Young People's Project
99 Bishop Allen Drive
Cambridge, MA 02139
(617) 354-8991
Website: http://www.typp.org
Facebook: @ypp
Twitter: @YPeoplesProject
The goal of this project to is empower young people with the skills and support they need to meet the challenges of their generation. They also strive to see that every young person regardless of class has access to high-quality education.

## WEBSITES

Because of the changing nature of internet links, Rosen Publishing has developed an online list of websites related to the subject of this book. This site is updated regularly. Please use this link to access this list:

http://www.rosenlinks.com/SPKUP/Class

# FOR FURTHER READING

Furgang, Kathy. *Ending Hunger and Homelessness Through Service Learning* (Service Learning for Teens). New York, NY: Rosen Publishing, 2015.

Gay, Kathlyn. *Bigotry and Intolerance: The Ultimate Teen Guide*. Lanham, MD: Scarecrow Press, 2013.

Gitlin, Marty. *Combatting Discrimination Against Women in the Gamer Community* (Combatting Shaming and Toxic Communities). New York, NY: Rosen Publishing, 2017.

Haugen, David M. *Discrimination* (Teen Rights and Freedoms). Farmington Hills, MI: Greenhaven Press, 2014.

Laine, Carolee. *The War on Poverty*. Minneapolis, MN: Essential Library, 2016.

Oachs, Emily Rose. *The Rising Cost of Education*. Minneapolis, MN: Essential Library, 2016.

Schab, Lisa M. *The Self-Esteem Workbook for Teens: Activities to Help You Build Confidence and Achieve Your Goals*. Oakland, CA: Instant Help, 2013.

Schlitz, Laura Amy. *The Hired Girl*. Somerville, MA: Candlewick Press, 2015.

Sheinmel, Courtney. *Edgewater*. New York, NY: Abrams Books, 2015.

# BIBLIOGRAPHY

Boucher, Christine. Interview with author. January 2017.

Cote, Stephanie, and Michael Kraus. "Crossing Class Lines." *New York Times*, October 3, 2014. https://www.nytimes.com/2014/10/05/opinion/sunday/crossing-financial-lanes.htm.

DeAngelis, Tori. "Class Differences." *Monitor on Psychology*, Volume 46, Number 2, p. 62, February 2015. American Psychological Association. http://www.apa.org/monitor/2015/02/class-differences.aspx.

"Discrimination: What Is It and How to Cope." American Psychological Association. Retrieved May 10, 2017. http://www.apa.org/helpcenter/discrimination.aspx.

Drier, Peter. "America's Classist Education System." *Huffington Post*, July 25, 2014. http://www.huffingtonpost.com/peter-dreier/americas-rigged-education_b_5621332.html.

Fisher, Daniel. "Poor Students Are the Real Victims of College Discrimination." *Forbes,* May 2, 2012. https://www.forbes.com/sites/danielfisher/2012/05/02/poor-students-are-the-real-victims-of-college-discrimination/#47a21fc5610e.

Gammon, Katherine. "How Money Shapes Young Minds." *Good Health*, January 27, 2017. https://health.good.is/features/education-word-gap-rich-poor.

Horsely, Scott. "The Income Gap: Unfair, or Are We Just Jealous." NPR, January 4, 2012. http://www.npr.org/2012/01/14/145213421/the-income-gap-unfair-or-are-we-just-jealous.

Long, Heather. "We Should Be Talking About Class in America as Much as Race Issues." *Guardian*, August 28, 2013. https://www.theguardian.com/

commentisfree/2013/aug/28/martin-luther-king
-poverty-message.

Name withheld. Interview with author. January 2017.

Payne, Ruby K. *A Framework for Understanding Poverty: A Cognitive Approach.* Highlands, TX: aha! Process, 2013.

Tough, Paul. "The Class-Consciousness Raiser." *New York Times Magazine*, June 10, 2007. http://www.nytimes .com/2007/06/10/magazine/10payne-t.html.

University of California Counseling and Psychological Services. "Addressing Racism and Discrimination: Considerations for Ally's." Retrieved May 16, 2017. http://caps.ucsc.edu/pdf/coping-with-racism.pdf.

University of Wisconsin School of Medicine and Public Health. "Social Class Discrimination Contributes to Poorer Health," June 15, 2012. http://www.med.wisc .edu/news-events/social-class-discrimination -contributes-to-poorer-health/38020.

Urban, Beth. Interview with author. January 2017.

Wellington, Sam. "Staggering Along the Periphery: Classism in America." *Dissident Voice*, August 19, 2010. http:// dissidentvoice.org/2010/08/staggering-along-the -periphery-classism-in-america.

Williams, Joan C. "What So Many People Don't Get About the U.S. Working Class." *Harvard Business Review*, November 10, 2016. https://hbr.org/2016/11/what-so -many-people-dont-get-about-the-u-s-working-class?utm _source=digg&utm_medium=email.

Wing, Nick. "Here's the Painful Truth About What It Means to Be Working Poor in America." *Huffington Post*, May 19, 2014. http://www.huffingtonpost.com/2014/05/19 /working-poor-stories_n_5297694.html.

# INDEX

# ABOUT THE AUTHOR

Sherri Mabry Gordon's passion is to provide young people with information about issues and interests that impact their lives. She has written books dealing with bullying, public shaming, technology, relationship, food allergies, and many other relevant issues. Currently, she is working on young adult fiction and writing regularly about bullying and patient empowerment for Verywell.com, where she is the bullying prevention expert.

# PHOTO CREDITS

Cover Frederic J. Brown/AFP/Getty Images; pp. 4–5 (background) igorstevanovic/Shutterstock.com; p. 5 (inset) oneinchpunch/Shutterstock.com; p. 6 Monkey Business Images/Shutterstock.com; pp. 7, 18, 29, 39, 46, 81/Shutterstock.com; p. 8 Moviestore collection Ltd/Alamy Stock Photo; p. 11 Kevork Djansezian/Getty Images; p. 15 United Archives GmbH/Alamy Stock Photo; p. 19 Blend Images/Shutterstock.com; p. 21 monkeybusinessimages/iStock/Thinkstock; p. 22 David McNew/Getty Images; p. 25 BananaStock/Thinkstock; p. 30 Entertainment Pictures/Alamy Stock Photo; p. 32 The Washington Post/Getty Images; p. 35 Library of Congress Prints and Photographs Division; p. 37 © AP Images; p. 40 Archive Photos/Moviepix/Getty Images; p. 42 Pacific Press/LightRocket/Getty Images; p. 44 © Jeff Newman/Globe Photos/ZUMA Press; p. 47 © iStockphoto.com/kali9; p. 49 Mark Metcalfe/Getty Images; p. 51 Photo 12/Alamy Stock Photo.

Design: Michael Moy; Layout: Nicole Russo-Duca; Editor: Carolyn DeCarlo; Photo Research: Nicole DiMella